1 FACTS

SHEFFIELD UTD

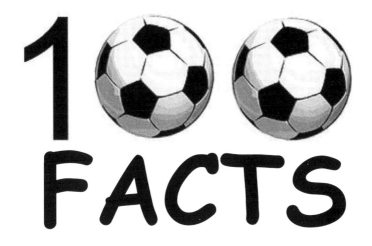

100 FACTS

SHEFFIELD UTD

Steve Horton

WYMER
WP
PUBLISHING
Bedford, England

First published in Great Britain in 2020
by Wymer Publishing
www.wymerpublishing.co.uk
Wymer Publishing is a trading name of Wymer (UK) Ltd

978-1-912782-45-1

Edited by Jerry Bloom.

Typeset and Design by Andy Bishop / 1016 Sarpsborg
Printed and bound by CMP, Poole, Dorset

A catalogue record for this book is available from the British Library.

Sketches by Becky Welton. © 2014.

1889
SHEFFIELD UNITED
CRICKET CLUB

Sheffield United was formed by members of Sheffield United Cricket Club, who saw football as a way of generating income during the winter months.

The cricket club was formed in 1854 and took over the lease at Bramall Lane the following year. As well as hosting cricket matches, Bramall Lane was used as a venue for football. It became Sheffield Wednesday's home ground in 1880 and they stayed until 1887 when they moved to Olive Grove.

On 22nd March 1889, six days after Bramall Lane hosted an FA Cup semi-final between Preston and West Bromwich Albion, members of the cricket club met at 10 Norfolk Row, the offices of the ground committee. Having seen the potential income football could bring, they decided to form a club named Sheffield United.

Ironically it was at the suggestion of the club president Sir Charles Clegg, who was on the Board of Wednesday, that United was formed. The following week, advertisements were placed in the local press inviting potential players to get in touch with secretary Mr Wostinholm.

United's first game on 7th September 1889 was a 4-1 defeat against Notts Rangers at Meadow Lane. Two weeks later they played at Bramall Lane for the first time, losing 4-0 to Birmingham St Georges.

1890
RECORD
13-0 DEFEAT

Sheffield United's first season in the FA Cup saw them thrashed 13-0 by Bolton Wanderers in the second round, which remains a club record defeat.

In the first round United beat Football League side Burnley 2-1 at Bramall Lane. They were then paired with Bolton Wanderers at home, but had to switch the tie to their Pikes Lane ground to avoid clashing with Sheffield Wednesday's home game.

United struggled on a heavy pitch and were 5-0 down at half-time. Calder, United's centre forward, had a torrid time and on many occasions slipped as he was lining up to shoot.

The *Sheffield Daily Telegraph* reported that during the second period, all of the play with the exception of a few minutes took place in the United half. Bolton rattled in eight more goals, four of them scored by Jim Cassidy. The paper reported that United's keeper Charlie Howlett did not play badly, it was simply a case of their forwards being unable to mount any sustained periods of attack.

Bolton went on to reach that season's semi-finals, where they were beaten by United's neighbours Wednesday.

1890
THE FIRST
STEEL CITY DERBY

The first time the two clubs met in what became known as the Steel City Derby, Sheffield United were narrowly beaten by Sheffield Wednesday.

After some initial friction due to Wednesday's move from Bramall Lane, relations between the two clubs improved during 1890. It was agreed to play two exhibition matches, the first of which took place at Wednesday's Olive Grove ground on 15th December that year.

On a frosty day, United had the better of the first half. After twenty minutes they took the lead when Robertson, whose first name was not recorded, reacted quickest following a corner. Wednesday tried their best to equalise before half-time but Charlie Howlett in the United goal made three fine saves.

Early in the second half William Hodder headed Wednesday's equalising goal. Buoyed by this, they continued to attack but United's defence held firm. After weathering this storm, it was an even game and United's Bernard Shaw rued mishitting a shot when he had a great chance.

With five minutes remaining United failed to properly clear a corner and Harry Winterbottom made it 2-1 to Wednesday. There was still time to chase an equaliser but when United were awarded a free kick in a good position, they failed to make it count.

Four weeks later the teams met again at Bramall Lane, with United levelling it up by winning 3-2.

1891
MIDLAND LEAGUE
TO NORTHERN LEAGUE

FACT **4**

In 1891 Sheffield United joined the Northern League after just one season in the Midland League.

United finished fifth out of ten teams in the 1890-91 season. In the second half of the season they recruited established professionals in readiness for a switch to a higher level.

In the summer of 1891 United sought election to the Football League but did not get enough votes. They instead joined the highly competitive Northern League, which contained a number of professional teams. There was a lot more travelling involved, with the nearest opponents Darlington being more than eighty miles away.

Secretary J. B. Wostinholm continued to recruit players who were professionals and had experience at a higher level. United had a great start to the season, winning their first four games. They eventually finished third, behind Middlesbrough and champions Middlesbrough Ironopolis. United were the leagues joint top scorers, with 49 goals from sixteen matches.

For the 1892-93 season the Football League expanded with the creation of the Second Division. This time United's application was successful, although they were still angered by Sheffield Wednesday being elected straight to the First Division.

1892
RECORD
AWAY VICTORY

Sheffield United's record away victory was a huge 10-0 win at Port Vale in a Second Division fixture on 10th December 1892.

Vale had some key players, including their regular keeper, out injured. On a snow-covered pitch, John Drummond opened the scoring after just two minutes. Sandy Wallace doubled the lead a minute later and Harry Hammond made it 3-0 after six minutes.

Vale's keeper made two good saves before Arthur Watson got the fourth goal after eleven minutes. The same player made it 5-0 after half an hour and it remained that way at half-time.

Three minutes after the restart Hammond scored a sixth and Fred Davies struck twice in two minutes to make it 8-0 with just an hour gone. Hammond completed his hat-trick with the ninth goal and with ten minutes remaining he scored again to take United into double figures.

The remainder of the game was more even, partly due to United being reduced to ten men as a player went off injured.

The following Saturday the two sides met again at Bramall Lane, when Vale had their injured players back. Despite this United still had a comfortable 4-0 win.

1893
PROMOTED
AFTER A TEST MATCH

Sheffield United won promotion to the First Division in 1892-93, thanks to a test match victory against Accrington.

United were unbeaten at Bramall Lane and finished second in the table, a point behind Small Heath (now Birmingham City). However there was no automatic promotion and relegation, with the top teams from the Second Division playing test matches against the bottom sides from the top flight.

Nottingham was the neutral venue for United's test match against Accrington and several hundred fans travelled there on two charter trains. They were given a boost with the news that captain Billy Hendry, who had been an injury doubt, was passed fit to play.

The first half was end to end and only poor shooting from the forwards of both sides kept the score at 0-0 after 45 minutes.

Ten minutes after the restart John Drummond went on a solo run and scored with a fierce shot to put United ahead. United then had to defend deep to fend off Accrington's attacks. Drummond showed his worth at the back too, making a goal line clearance. Goalkeeper Charlie Howlett made a couple of important saves as United held on for victory.

United went up along with Darwen, who beat Notts County, but top Second Division side Small Heath lost out, losing to Newton Heath (later Manchester United).

1898
FIRST DIVISION
CHAMPIONS

Sheffield United won the Football League Championship for the first time in 1897-98, clinching the title in their penultimate game at Bolton.

After finishing second the previous season, United were unbeaten in their first fourteen games of 1897-98, building up a healthy lead. There was a dip in form after Christmas but a 1-0 win over closest challengers Sunderland on 2nd April meant the title destiny stayed in their own hands with two games left.

United knew that they could clinch the title on 8th April if they won at Bolton and Sunderland failed to beat Bury. Several hundred fans took a Great Central excursion train and were in fine voice amongst a crowd of 20,000.

There was an early blow when Fred Priest picked up an injury, but he was able to return to action after ten minutes. Midway through the first half Ernest Needham put United ahead with a great shot from the left of the penalty area. There was no further scoring and with the news that Bury had beaten Sunderland, United were confirmed as champions.

United earned praise nationwide for their efforts. The *London Globe* commented "They have thoroughly deserved their honour. They have, taking the season through, proved themselves the best team in England".

1898
SHERIFF OF
LONDON CHARITY SHIELD

In 1898 Sheffield United played for the Sheriff of London Charity Shield, a one-off game that eventually became the Community Shield.

The contest was proposed by Sir Thomas Dewar, Sheriff of London, who wanted to see England's best professional and amateur sides face each other with the proceeds going to charity. United, who had a healthy lead in the First Division, were invited to take part in a match against leading amateur side Corinithians.

The match took place at Crystal Palace on 19th March in front of a crowd of 20,000. After a poor first half, Corinthians had the better of the play after the break, but United's defence remained firm and the game ended 0-0.

The replay took place on a Monday, meaning a reduced crowd of 8,000. John Almond gave United a first half lead but after an hour Corinthians equalised from a free kick. The game finished 1-1 and as United didn't want to play extra time, the trophy was shared.

The Sheriff of London Charity Shield was played until 1907, but the Football Association took over the competition when amateur clubs broke away. It was renamed the Community Shield in 2002. United's participation in 1898 remains the only time they have been involved.

1899
A MARATHON
CUP SEMI-FINAL

Sheffield United needed four games, one of which was abandoned, to overcome Liverpool in the 1899 FA Cup semi-final.

The first game took place at Nottingham on 18th March and was evenly matched. United scored first through George Hedley but Liverpool hit back to lead 2-1 by half-time. Midway through the second half, Ernest Needham equalised to earn United a deserved draw.

The replay five days later in Bolton was even more entertaining than the first game. United were 1-0 down at half-time and fell further behind five minutes after the restart. Goals from Billy Beer and Walter Bennet pulled it back to 2-2 only for Liverpool to score two more. With six minutes to go United looked to be out but Fred Priest scored twice to force a 4-4 draw.

The third game was at Fallowfield in Manchester. Due to continued crowd encroachment onto the pitch, which caused the first half to last over ninety minutes, the game was abandoned with the score 1-0 to Liverpool.

On 30th March at Derby the sides met for a fourth time. With just five minutes left and extra time looming, Beer scored what proved to be the decisive goal, taking United to their first FA Cup final.

1899
FOUR SECOND HALF
GOALS WIN THE CUP

FACT **10**

After finally overcoming Liverpool in the last four, Sheffield United made no mistake in the final. They beat Derby County 4-1 at Crystal Palace, all the goals coming in the second half.

A heavy downpour before kick-off meant the pitch was heavy when the game started. United struggled and fell behind in the twelfth minute to a goal by John Boag. Stephen Bloomer then missed two good chances to further Derby's lead.

Towards the end of the first half there were signs that United were getting back into the game. After the restart the sun was shining and the pitch far easier to play on. With an hour gone, Walter Bennett headed an equaliser to the delight of United's supporters. Three minutes later Billy Beer put United ahead, reacting swiftly after the Derby keeper could only parry his first effort.

Derby were now struggling, their first half efforts having tired them out. With twenty minutes remaining Jack Almond scored from Bennett's cross and there was no doubt the cup was coming to Sheffield. Towards the end of the game Derby were reduced to ten men through injury and Fred Priest got United's fourth a minute from full time.

United's players then spent a few days at leisure in London, before returning to Sheffield three days later for a victorious homecoming parade.

1900
22 GAMES UNBEATEN
STILL NOT ENOUGH

Sheffield United enjoyed an unbeaten run of 22 games during 1899-1900, but it still wasn't enough to win the Football League Championship.

United opened the season with five straight wins during September before drawing 2-2 with Sunderland. At the end of October, they were four points clear of Aston Villa, who they had beaten 2-1 at Bramall Lane in the tenth game.

The unbeaten run continued in November and December. They ended the year with an impressive 5-0 home win over Everton. They were now six points ahead of Villa, who had a game in hand. United's first game of 1900 was a 1-1 draw at home to Derby, extending the run to 22 games. It finally came to an end on 20th January, with a 2-1 loss to Bury at Gigg Lane.

Winning the title remained in United's hands until Easter when they drew two games in succession. This meant they were two points adrift of behind Villa who had played a game more but had a superior goal average.

Villa had completed their fixtures before United travelled to Burnley for their final game on 23rd April, needing an unlikely 8-0 win to secure the title. They lost 1-0 to finish the season in second place, two points behind Villa and seven ahead of third place Sunderland.

1901
AN FA CUP
FINAL SHOCK

Sheffield United were shocked in the 1901 FA Cup final, losing to the then non-league Tottenham Hotspur.

United had a tough run to the final, beating First Division opposition in every round. Their opponents for the final were Tottenham, who played in the Southern League. They had knocked out three top-flight teams on their way to the final, which was played at Crystal Palace on 20th April.

The game was watched by a huge crowd of over 110,000. Fred Priest gave United the lead after ten minutes but Sandy Brown equalised midway through the first half and it remained 1-1 at the break. After six minutes of the second half Brown scored again, only for Walter Bennett to head United's equaliser soon afterwards.

The replay took place at Burnden Park in Bolton a week later, the FA ignoring requests from both sides for it to take place in Birmingham. United spent a few days in preparation at Lytham on the Lancashire coast.

In front of a disappointing crowd of 20,000 Priest put United ahead five minutes before half-time. However after the break Tottenham scored three times without reply to condemn United to a shock defeat.

1902
FA CUP
WINNERS

The disappointment of losing the 1901 FA Cup final was made up by lifting the trophy the following year.

United beat Northampton, Bolton and Newcastle in the early rounds, then needed two replays to get past Derby County in the semi-final. Their opponents for the final at Crystal Palace on 19th April were Southampton, who like Tottenham the previous year were a non-league side.

In front of 74,000 fans Alf Common gave United the lead early in the second half. However with United looking set for victory, Southampton equalised thanks to a late goal from Harry Wood, the referee dismissing appeals for offside. United keeper William Foulke was said to be so incensed he went looking for the referee, who locked himself in a broom cupboard to escape his anger.

The two sides were back at Crystal Palace for the replay a week later. It was a bitterly cold day and United went ahead after just two minutes, George Hedley capitalising from a goalkeeping error.

Southampton enjoyed most of the play from then on and deserved their equaliser, which came midway through the second half. With extra time looming, Billy Barnes scored what turned out to be the winner when defenders failed to cut out a cross. It meant United had won the cup for a second time.

FACT 14

1902 TEST MATCH

United's Bramall Lane ground, which still hosted county cricket, was the venue for a Test match in the summer of 1902.

The match was the third of a five match Ashes series between England and Australia. The first two Tests in Birmingham and London had been drawn.

Australia won the toss and elected to bat, scoring 194 in their first innings. At close of play on the first day England were 102-5 but they collapsed on the second, adding just 43 to that total to be all out for 145.

In their second innings, Australia's Clem Hill hit a century as they built up a big lead, eventually being all out for 289. This left England needing 339 to win, a total no country had achieved to win a Test at that time.

England started their second innings well enough and were 73-1 at the end of play on the second day. However, just like in the first innings, they fell apart in the morning and lost three wickets in half an hour. They were eventually bowled out for 195, meaning Australia won by 143 runs.

This turned out to be the one and only Test to be played at Bramall Lane, although the ground did host a touring side from India in 1946.

1905
FATTY FOULKE
LEAVES

15

William 'Fatty' Foulke, who had been Sheffield United's keeper for the past eleven years, left the club in 1904 after turning down a new contract.

Foulke joined United in 1894 and even at six feet two inches he was tall for a goalkeeper. He towered above his teammates in an age when the average male height was less than five and a half feet.

He was also around twice the weight of most other players. For a man of his size, Foulke was extremely agile. During 1896-97 United had the best defensive record in the league and he earned his one and only England cap. Foulke was not popular with the football authorities, due to his tendency to argue with referees and pull on the crossbar to make the goal smaller.

Foulke won one Football League Championship and two FA Cups with United. He was a colossus in goal, a good shot stopper and also had the ability to kick and punch the ball far upfield. An all-round sportsman, he played four county cricket matches for Derbyshire in 1900.

Each season Foulke's weight increased, leading to taunts from both sets of fans. By 1904 he was over twenty stone and having difficulty getting down to low shots. After appearing in just ten games in 1904-05 he left and joined Chelsea, newly elected to the Second Division.

FACT 16

1907
THE
BLADES

Sheffield United didn't claim the nickname of Blades until 1907, eighteen years after they were founded.

The origins of steelmaking in Sheffield date back to the fourteenth century, while in 1624 the Company of Cutlers in Hallamshire was formed to promote Sheffield's steel around the world.

Inexpensive mass production became possible in the mid 1800s with the invention of the Bessemer Converter. Sir Henry Bessemer moved his steel making business from Hertfordshire to Sheffield to be at the heart of the industry.

Sheffield's location, surrounded by hills that provided the raw materials and rivers to generate power, made it ideal for steel production. By the beginning of the nineteenth century the city was producing over 95% of the United Kingdom's steel.

For some time, United and Wednesday were both nicknamed the Blades or the Cutlers, referring to this dominance.

However with the FA Cup looming in 1907, a national cartoonist referred to United as the Blades and Wednesday as the Owls, due to their ground being in the district of Owlerton. From then on, the nickname of the Blades became unique to United.

1910
ERNEST NEEDHAM
RETIRES

Sheffield United's first superstar, Ernest Needham, retired from playing in 1910 after nineteen years with the club.

Needham was eighteen when he joined the club, then in the Northern League, in 1891. After being elected to the Football League in 1892, he scored five times in twenty appearances as they won promotion.

In 1895 Needham was appointed captain of United and led the club to some of their greatest triumphs. Under his guidance they won the First Division title and two FA Cups. Needham was solidly built, strong in the tackle and a good distributor of the ball. His talents were recognised by the FA, who selected him sixteen times for England, whom he captained once.

It wasn't just football where Needham had talent. For ten years he played cricket for Derbyshire, once hitting a century in both innings of the match.

Needham's last appearance for United was at Bolton on 22nd January 1910. He had made over 500 appearances for the club, whose fans had nicknamed him 'Nudger.' He remained at Bramall Lane as a scout and could be seen at games until just a few weeks before his death in 1936 aged 63.

1912
BRAMALL LANE
HOSTS CUP FINAL

Bramall Lane is one of only two venues that have hosted both an FA Cup final and cricket Test match.

The 1912 FA Cup final at Crystal Palace on 20th April 1912 between Barnsley and West Bromwich Albion finished in a 0-0 draw. Four days later the replay took place at Bramall Lane, with most of the 38,555 crowd making the short journey from Barnsley.

It was hot and sunny when the game kicked off at 3pm. Despite the conditions it was a hard-fought game in which Albion had the upper hand against their Second Division opponents. Barnsley did come close to scoring though when the keeper fumbled Wilf Bartrop's shot but a covering defender cleared the danger.

The score was 0-0 after ninety minutes and extra time was required. Albion continued to dominate but with two minutes remaining Harry Tufnell broke clear and scored with a hard and low shot that was out of the keeper's reach.

After the game Barnsley's motor coach was cheered as it drove through the streets of Sheffield. The players were given a heroes' welcome when they reached Barnsley.

The Oval in London is the only other ground to host both an FA Cup final and Test match.

FACT 19

1915
THE KHAKI
CUP FINAL

Sheffield United won the FA Cup in 1915. The final is commonly referred to as the Khaki Cup Final, due to the large numbers of uniformed soldiers attending.

War had broken out in 1914 at the start of the season but the football authorities opted, despite much criticism, to continue with organised competition. United beat Blackpool, Liverpool, Bradford Park Avenue, Oldham and Bolton to reach the final where they faced Chelsea.

The match was played at Old Trafford, Manchester to avoid travel disruption in London. Due to restrictions on movement and the number of men called up by the forces, the attendance of 49,557 was down on previous finals. Those watching included many wearing their army uniforms, some of them having been wounded in action.

United were clear favourites against a Chelsea side battling relegation. The first half was one sided and only the fine form of Chelsea's keeper kept United from scoring until James Simmons finally broke the deadlock on 36 minutes.

The second half was ruined somewhat by thick fog. There was very little goalmouth action until the closing stages, when goals from Stanley Fazackerley and Joe Kitchen secured a 3-0 victory for United.

United were presented with the cup by the Earl of Derby, who urged all to "join together and play a sterner game for England".

1916
HARRY
JOHNSON

Sheffield United's all-time record goalscorer is Harry Johnson, who joined the club as a teenager in 1916.

Johnson was a former Barnsley Grammar School pupil whose father, also Harry, played for the Blades between 1895 and 1909. He joined the club in 1916 soon after his seventeenth birthday.

After just a handful of wartime games the *Star Green 'Un* predicted that Johnson "gives promise of developing into as good a player as his father". Before that could come about his country needed him and he enlisted with the Royal Engineers, serving with a trench mortar unit in France.

When the Football League resumed, Johnson was prolific. In the eight seasons between 1920-21 and 1928-29, he was United's leading scorer in eight of them.

Johnson lost his place as United's centre forward due to the emergence of Jimmy Dunne. At the end of 1930-31 he moved to Mansfield, who were then in the Third Division. He had scored what remains a record 201 goals for the Blades in 313 league appearances, all of them in the First Division.

Despite the drop in standard, Johnson's appetite for the game remained as great as ever and he scored 104 goals in 163 games for Mansfield before retiring in 1935.

FACT 21

1925
WEMBLEY
FA CUP WINNERS

Sheffield United's first visit to Wembley Stadium in 1925, saw them triumph against Cardiff City in the FA Cup final.

United reached the final by beating Corinthians, Sheffield Wednesday, Everton, West Bromwich Albion and Southampton. Their opponents were Cardiff, the first Welsh side to reach the FA Cup final.

This was the third final to be played at Wembley, which had been completed in 1923. The match was an all ticket affair and United's supporters were outnumbered in the crowd of 91,763.

United's inside right was Tommy Boyle, whose father Peter had played for the club in the finals of 1899, 1901 and 1902. Of the 1915 cup final team, only Billy Cook remained.

Fred Tunstall gave United the lead after half an hour, latching onto a long ball and shooting past Tom Farquharson. It turned out to be the only goal of the game, in which United were rarely threatened by Cardiff.

United remained in London and enjoyed a day out at Windsor on the Sunday. They then returned home to a heroes' welcome. Tens of thousands turned out to see the players parade the cup from the balcony of the Town Hall, where they were joined by the Lord Mayor.

The club's most prolific season for goals scored was in 1925-26. A total of 102 were amassed, an incredible 72 of those at Bramall Lane.

United failed to win any of their first seven games, but still scored in all of them. This included a 7-4 defeat at Bury. Their first victory didn't come until the first weekend of October, when Birmingham City were beaten 4-1 at Bramall Lane.

The victory over Birmingham was the start of run of seven successive home wins, one of which was an 8-3 thrashing of Manchester City. On Christmas Day, United lost 4-2 at home to Leicester. However they made up for this in style on New Years Day with an 11-2 rout of Cardiff.

Other big home wins were 6-1 over Burnley and 4-0 against Arsenal. United finished fifth in the league, partly due to their away form which saw only four wins from 21 games, scoring thirty goals.

United's final home record was won fifteen, drew three and lost three. They scored in every game at Bramall Lane and their total of 72 home goals was 22 more than champions Huddersfield.

The leading United scorer during the campaign with 23 goals in all competitions was Harry Johnson, who topped the club goal charts in eight out of the ten seasons of that decade.

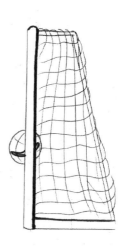

1926
SHEFFIELD UNITED
SCORE ELEVEN

The only time The Blades have scored eleven goals in a game was against Cardiff City on New Year's Day 1926.

On a heavy pitch with rain continuing to fall heavily, United adapted the better of the two sides and kept the ball off the ground as much as possible. They were 2-0 up after 22 minutes but Cardiff pulled a goal back after half an hour.

United moved into a healthy lead before half-time, scoring three times in a ten minute spell without reply. Two of the goals were due to errors by the Cardiff keeper, who failed to hold on to the wet ball.

With eight minutes of the second half gone United went 6-1 ahead. Cardiff's plight was then worsened when they were reduced to ten men due to injury and within four minutes it was 7-1. It was a quarter of an hour before United scored again, but this was the first of three in four minutes that took the score to 10-1.

Harry Johnson completed United's scoring with ten minutes left and shortly before the end Cardiff pulled it back to 11-2. Both Johnson and Mercer got hat-tricks, Boyle and Gillespie two each, with Tunstall scoring the other.

1927
THE FIRST LIVE
RADIO COMMENTARY

FACT **24**

Sheffield United were involved in a piece of broadcasting history on 22nd January 1927 when their game at Arsenal was the first football match to have radio commentary.

That month the BBC were given a charter allowing them to broadcast major sporting events. The first commentator was former rugby union international Henry Wakelam, whose selection process involved commentating on a school game.

For the assistance of listeners, a diagram of the pitch divided into eight squares was published in the Radio Times. Wakelam would often refer to where the ball was so listeners could visualise the action.

An hour before kick-off the game was in doubt due to a frozen pitch, but it went ahead after the spreading of salt and sand. Both sets of players struggled to adapt to the now slushy conditions with the ball also getting stuck in sand on occasions.

After the break the players had got to grips with the situation better. With ten minutes remaining Charlie Buchan reacted first in a goalmouth scramble to put Arsenal ahead. Three minutes later United were level thanks to Billy Gillespie's header from a corner.

The *Sheffield Daily Telegraph* was reasonably complimentary of the broadcast. It stated that sometimes Wakelam talked too fast, but those who knew the teams would have enjoyed following the action.

1927
HARRY JOHNSON
SCORES FIVE

The only Sheffield United player to score five goals in a top-flight game was Harry Johnson, in a 6-2 win over West Ham United on Boxing Day 1927.

On a snow-covered pitch, Fred Tunstall scored the first goal in the third minute after being set up by Johnson. Just seven minutes later, Johnson scored the rebound after Tunstall's shot hit the post.

Shortly before half-time West Ham got a goal back but early in the second period United, or more specifically Johnson, took control. In the fiftieth minute he seized on a mistake to make it 3-1 then five minutes later headed in from a corner to complete his hat-trick.

There was still less than an hour of the game gone when Johnson hit an unstoppable shot to score his fourth. Around the 65th minute he got his fifth, stooping to head in a cross and putting United 6-1 up. That completed his side's scoring and West Ham got a consolation shortly before the end.

Afterwards, Johnson learned that his brother Tommy had scored four goals for his amateur team. The following day the sides met again at West Ham's Boleyn Ground. Johnson opened the scoring after just two minutes but the windy conditions made play difficult and the game finished 1-1.

The only time Sheffield United have won by a ten-goal margin in the top division was on 19th January 1929 when they beat Burnley 10-0 at Bramall Lane.

Only a week before this game, United had been beaten 2-1 by Burnley in the FA Cup at their Turf Moor ground. Earlier in the season United had also lost by that scoreline when the two sides met at Burnley in the First Division.

For this fixture at Bramall Lane, the Blades were boosted by the return of leading scorer Harry Johnson, who had been injured for the cup tie. He showed just what his teammates had been missing when he scored both goals to give United a 2-0 half-time lead.

Four minutes after the restart Johnson completed his hat-trick. The Blades added four more in a twenty-minute spell; two came from Fred Tunstall and the others from Johnson and Tom Phillipson.

With thirteen minutes to go Billy Gillespie headed the eighth. Sidney Gibson made it 9-0 with a great strike and Phillipson dribbled through unchallenged to take it to double figures with two minutes remaining.

1931
JIMMY DUNNE'S

41 GOALS IN A SEASON

The most goals scored in a single season by a Sheffield United player was 41 by Jimmy Dunne in 1930-31.

Irishman Dunne had signed for United from New Brighton in 1926 but he had to wait patiently for his chance. He finally became a regular in 1929-30 and set a club scoring record of 36 goals, beating Harry Johnson's 33 of two seasons earlier.

Dunne's 41 goals in 1930-31 helped United finish in fifteenth, an improvement on the previous season when they only avoided relegation on goal average.

Dunne scored five hat-tricks during the campaign. His most impressive haul was against Liverpool at Bramall Lane in April, when he scored all his side's goals in a 4-1 win.

Some journalists claimed that Dunne was the finest striker in England and perhaps the best header of the ball in the game. However the man himself was very modest about his achievements. In an interview with the *Star Green 'Un* in January, he heaped praise on United's wingers for their crossing skills, which he said made it so much easier for him to score.

When goals in the FA Cup and for Ireland were taken into account, his total for the season was fifty. No Irish player has scored as many goals in an English league season since.

FACT 28 TOP FLIGHT CONSECUTIVE SCORING RECORD

Jimmy Dunne's fine form continued in the 1931-32 season, when he set a record for scoring in consecutive games that still stands today.

Dunne's haul of 33 league goals was not as good as the season before but still enough to make him United's top scorer. However his feat of scoring in twelve consecutive games has never been equalled.

The goalscoring run started in October when Dunne got both goals in a 2-0 win at Grimsby. He then scored in each of the next ten games, of which six were won and four lost.

On New Year's Day Dunne scored in his twelfth successive gme, netting twice as United came from behind to beat Blackburn 3-2 at Bramall Lane. They then made the long journey to the south coast to face Portsmouth the following day. It turned out to be unlucky thirteen for Dunne, who failed to find the net as United lost 2-1.

No player has managed to match Dunne's achievement in the English top-flight. The closest to doing so was Leicester's Jamie Vardy when he scored in eleven successive games in 2015-16.

1932

FACT 29
TRAGIC DEATH OF
JOHN NICHOLSON

John Nicholson, Sheffield United's secretary for over thirty years, was tragically killed in 1932 shortly before the team set off for an away game.

Appointed in 1899, Nicholson was at the club for one Football League Championship success and four FA Cup triumphs. Although his title was secretary, he carried out many of the functions of the modern day manager. He was helped in his duties by a trainer, while the team was selected by a committee.

On the morning of 23rd April 1932, Nicholson was on his way to join the United party travelling to Birmingham where they were to play Aston Villa in a league match. After alighting a tram outside Midland Station, he was knocked down by a lorry and pronounced dead on arrival at the Royal Hospital.

The players were aware of the accident but only learned the full extent of it on arrival at Villa Park. They wore black armbands and a minute's silence was held before kick off, but it was not surprising that their minds were not focused and United lost 5-0.

The *Sheffield Independent* said that "in a secretarial and administrative capacity he had few superiors". It was estimated that a crowd of 6,000 attended his burial at Darnall Cemetery.

1933
RECORD
LEAGUE DEFEAT

Sheffield United's heaviest league defeat was a 10-3 thrashing at Middlesbrough on 18th November 1933.

United went ahead after just four minutes thanks to a 35 yard drive from Reg Baines. They had three chances to increase the lead before George Camsell equalised midway through the first half. Two minutes later Middlesbrough scored again through Charles Ferguson and on the half hour Camsell added another.

The *Star Green 'un* reporter described the home side as "like an avenging army". Fred Warren made it 4-1, then Robert Bruce hit the fifth from a free kick and soon after added the sixth. On the stroke of half-time Jack Pickering pulled one back for United with their first goal attempt since Middlesbrough's equaliser.

Eight minutes into the second half Camsell completed his hat-trick and on the hour Robert Baxter made it 8-2. With a quarter of an hour to go Baines scored another for United. Both teams were weary but Camsell still found strength to get his fourth with five minutes left. Bruce then completed his own hat-trick and took the score into double figures right on full-time.

A cruel irony of the 10-3 scoreline was that United had scored three goals for the first time that season but were defeated so heavily. The following week they beat Blackburn 1-0 at Bramall Lane but the season ended in relegation.

The lowest ever attendance for a league match at Bramall Lane was on 27th April 1935 when just 4,014 turned out for Sheffield United's Second Division game with Nottingham Forest.

This was the last home game of what had been an indifferent season for United, who eventually finished eleventh. Attendances had generally been 12-15,000 but for this fixture many fans made their disappointment known by staying away.

One factor behind the exceptionally low attendance was that fans had advance warning of four changes being made to the regular line-up. This was reported in the local press as necessary to help the management decide who should be retained for the following season.

Those who did attend saw United go ahead in the first minute when Jock Dodds scored after a fine pass by Mick Killourhy. After only seven minutes it was 2-0 thanks to another goal from Dodds, this one a header.

Forest pulled a goal back after 25 minutes and there was no further scoring. United did have plenty more chances though with one Killourhy shot hitting the bar. The game was far from an end of season affair with scintillating attacking play by United at times.

There has never been a lower league attendance at Bramall Lane since, although there have been lower crowds in minor cups.

Less than a year after just 4,014 fans watched a league game at Bramall Lane, the ground hosted its highest ever crowd. A massive 68,287 crammed in for an FA Cup fifth round tie with Leeds on 15th February 1936.

The Blades were enjoying a good season and pushing for promotion. In the previous round they defeated First Division Preston after a replay and interest in this tie was huge. The gates were closed ninety minutes before kick-off with thousands locked out, including plenty wearing Leeds colours.

Fans were entertained by the City Police Band as they waited patiently for kick-off. When the game did start many could not see what was happening due to fog.

United totally outplayed their First Division opponents, coming from a goal down to win 3-1 thanks to two from Jack Pickering and one from Jock Dodds. The only worry towards the end of the game was whether the referee would abandon it due to bad light.

Sadly the huge crowd did lead to 289 people requiring medical aid. One of those, a 56 year old Leeds fan, died in hospital while an elderly United fan collapsed in the street after the match.

1936
FA CUP AND PROMOTION HEARTBREAK

The 1935-36 season ended in huge disappointment for Sheffield United when they lost the FA Cup final and just missed out on promotion to the First Division.

United's opponents at Wembley on 25th April were Arsenal, who had been Football League champions four times so far that decade. However The Blades were not overawed in the first half which ended goalless and was an evenly matched affair.

In the second half, Arsenal's superior class shone through and with a quarter of an hour left Ted Drake gave them the lead. United almost equalised soon after but Jock Dodds' header came off the bar. United battled gallantly but were unable to force a replay.

After the match, there was further disappointing news for United when they learned the results of that day's Second Division games. Both Manchester United and Charlton had won, meaning only a freak set of results would see those teams fail to take the two promotion places.

Five days after the final, United could only draw 2-2 at bottom club Hull, who were already relegated to the Third Division North. United finished third in the table and would have to wait three more years for promotion.

1936
THE FIRST
FOREIGN TOUR

Sheffield United were one of the last top English clubs to go on tour. They did not play abroad until the summer of 1936, when they visited Denmark.

After completing their domestic fixtures, United's players were given three weeks off before their trip, which began from Sheffield Victoria station on the 25th May. The party consisted of sixteen players, manager Teddy Davison, trainer Billy Brelsford and three directors.

United arrived in Denmark as Wednesday were leaving, following three exhibition games against a Copenhagen Select XI. United started their trip in Aarhus, beating the local club there 8-2. They then had another high scoring game, winning 8-4 against Aalborg.

The party then moved on to the capital, where they lost 3-2 to a Copenhagen Select XI but beat a Danish Select XI 1-0. Next up was a 150-mile round trip to the southern city of Nykobing, where they won 5-1 against a regional select side. The tour was rounded off on 8th June, when a Danish Select XI were again beaten 1-0 in Copenhagen.

The tour had proved a great success, with huge crowds of 20,000 watching the games in Copenhagen. The players arrived back tanned, with Davison telling reporters they had all enjoyed themselves.

1939
FACT 35 WAR STOPS FIRST DIVISION RETURN

Sheffield United finally won promotion back to the First Division in 1938-39. However the outbreak of World War Two led to the suspension of the Football League after just three games.

United were unbeaten in their first six games and second in the table at Christmas. At the end of February they were comfortably placed but three successive defeats in March meant there was a lot of work to do.

During April, United played eight times, winning five and drawing three. They knew that a draw or victory in their last game against Tottenham at Bramall Lane on 6th May would be enough to secure promotion at the expense of Wednesday, who had completed their fixtures.

United made no mistake, cruising into a 4-0 half-time lead. They eventually won 6-1, easing off in the last twenty minutes. After the game the players appeared in the directors' box where they were cheered by thousands of fans on the pitch.

United started the 1939-40 season well and were in second place after three games when World War Two broke out. The Football League was immediately suspended and didn't resume until 1946.

1940
THE
SHEFFIELD BLITZ

During the Sheffield Blitz in December 1940, Bramall Lane was badly damaged by the German Airforce, known as the Luftwaffe.

Sheffield was heavily bombed over the nights of 12th and 15th December. Over 600 were killed and thousands of homes destroyed as the German government pursued a policy they hoped would demoralise the population of British cities.

At Bramall Lane the John Street grandstand took a direct hit, causing half of the roof to fall in and a floodlight pylon to collapse. There was also some damage to the Kop and the football pitch was left with two huge bomb craters. A scheduled Christmas Day fixture with Sheffield Wednesday was immediately switched to Hillsborough.

After clearing the debris from the pitch, filling in the craters and laying new turf, United were able to resume regional league fixtures there in September 1941. Addressing the damage to the grandstand was on hold until after the war and both sets of players had to change in the same dressing rooms.

The Blitz caused an unexpected postponement to a United game 45 years later. On 8th February 1985 an unexploded bomb was found in nearby Lancing Road where a new housing estate was being developed. Due to the risk to public safety, United's home game with Oldham was called off.

1946
FOOTBALL LEAGUE
NORTH CHAMPIONS

FACT **37**

Sheffield United were the champions of the Football League North in 1945-46.

After the suspension of the Football League in 1939, it was reorganised on a regional basis in 1940. However games were very ad hoc with teams playing fixtures only against local sides, with not everyone in the league necessarily playing each other.

For 1945-46, with the war over but many players still away with the forces, a proper format was adopted and all 22 teams played each other home and away. United enjoyed local derbies against Sheffield Wednesday, Barnsley and Chesterfield, with further afield fixtures being Blackpool and Newcastle.

The title was secured on 27th April. Although the Blades lost to Manchester City at Maine Road, closest challengers Everton were also beaten. United finished the season in first place with sixty points, five ahead of Everton who had been champions in 1939. They scored an incredible 112 goals.

United were then invited to play a Combined Services XI in the German capital Berlin, which was occupied by the Allied forces. The number of quality players still serving was shown by the fact United lost 5-1 in front of 10,000 fans at the Olympic Stadium.

1947
SHEFFIELD UTD DECIDE
THE TITLE IN JUNE

Sheffield United couldn't build on their wartime regional league success. However they did play a massive part in the destination of the Football League Championship in 1946-47, a season which continued until the middle of June.

That winter was one of the worst on record, causing many games to be postponed. United were particularly affected and played just four league games in the first ten weeks of 1947. This led to the season being extended beyond May to avoid teams playing on successive days.

The season was finally set to come to an end on 14th June, when United faced Stoke City at Bramall Lane. Stoke knew that if they could beat United, they would be champions. Any other result would hand the title to Liverpool, who had completed their fixtures two weeks earlier.

United were so hit by injuries that they had to recall 38 year old John Pickering for his first appearance of the season. The veteran scored the opening goal after just three minutes and although Stoke equalised soon afterwards, United went ahead again early in the second half through Walter Rickett.

Stoke were unable to overcome a stubborn United defence and it meant Liverpool, who were playing a Liverpool Senior Cup final at the same time, were the champions.

1948
FACT 39
JACK SMITH'S 203 APPEARANCES

Between 1935 and 1948, goalkeeper Jack Smith made an incredible 203 consecutive appearances for Sheffield United.

A likeable man who always had a grin on his face, Smith was nicknamed 'Smiler'. He joined United in 1930 after a successful trial period with the reserves and made seven first team appearances that season.

Smith's consecutive run of games started in the 1935-36 season and ended during 1947-48. He was then an ever present between 1936-37 and 1946-47, four seasons in total. He also played all three games of the abandoned 1939-40 season.

At the end of the 1948-49 season, when Smith played 23 league games, he was transfer listed. In what he thought would be his last game for United, a county cup final at Barnsley, he was "chaired" from the field at fulltime by his teammates.

Smith was expected to go into coaching but United did a U-turn and offered him a contract for the 1949-50 season. He played mainly for the reserves but did make two first team appearances in the Second Division. He left the club at the end of the season after spending twenty years there.

1949
BLADES DOWN AS
FACT 40 YORKSHIRE RIVALS ESCAPE

In an extremely tight relegation battle, Sheffield United went down on the last day of the 1948-49 season, with two Yorkshire rivals staying up at their expense.

Unlike two seasons earlier when United played until the middle of June, this time there had been few postponements and all clubs played their final fixtures at the same time. With one game left, just two points separated the bottom four teams, meaning any two of them could go down.

The Blades, third from bottom, were at home to Newcastle and knew a win would keep them up. A draw or defeat would leave them hoping others slipped up.

At half-time, United were drawing 0-0. Both Preston and Middlesbrough were winning, meaning the Blades looked set to be going down on goal average, along with Huddersfield.

In the second half, the situation became worse when Huddersfield took the lead. Even though Middlesbrough were pegged back at Aston Villa, a draw would still not be enough. Try as they might they could not find a winner against a solid Newcastle defence. It meant that when all the results were known United were down along with Preston, while Huddersfield and Middlesbrough were safe.

FACT 41
0.008 OF A GOAL AWAY FROM PROMOTION

In one of the closest ever promotion battles, Sheffield United missed out by just 0.008 in 1949-50. To deepen the pain, it was Sheffield Wednesday who went up at their expense.

Throughout the season there was rarely any doubt that Tottenham would be promoted as champions. They were ten points clear at Christmas but the race to join them was far tighter. United were one of a dozen or more teams who had realistic hopes of claiming the second promotion spot.

After the last round of regular fixtures on 29th April United were in second place, having played their 42 games. They then had to wait a week to see if Wednesday, who were a point behind with one game to play at home to Tottenham, could overhaul them.

Wednesday would be promoted with a win or 0-0 draw. However if it was 2-2 United would go up instead. A 1-1 draw would mean the two sides were completely tied and the Football League announced a one-off game between the two would take place.

In a tense game, Tottenham didn't sit back and went for victory, but Wednesday's defence held firm. It finished 0-0 and United were 0.008 of a goal short. If there was any consolation, Wednesday came straight back down the following season.

1951
FACT 42
UNITED'S 7-3 DERBY WIN

The highest scoring Steel City Derby was on 8th September 1951 when, Sheffield United thrashed Sheffield Wednesday 7-3 in a Second Division fixture at Bramall Lane.

In front of a huge crowd of 52,045 Wednesday's Keith Thomas opened the scoring after just ninety seconds. United overcame this setback and struck back to lead 2-1 midway through the first half. Alf Ringstead and Harold Brook scored the goals for United, who were also disappointed to see Fred Furniss have a penalty saved.

After an hour Dennis Woodhead equalised for Wednesday. However in an incredible eleven minutes spell United scored four times with goals from Brook, Derek Hawksworth, Ringstead and Fred Smith.

Thomas pulled a goal back for Wednesday with three minutes left but there was still time for a comeback but Brook restored the four goal cushion. The 7-3 scoreline was fully justified as United were quicker and much more organised than Wednesday.

The win took United to the top of the table after six games. However they eventually finished the season in a disappointing eighth place. The four goal margin of victory remained a derby record until it was matched in 1979 when United were beaten 4-0 at Wednesday

1952
FACT 43 SEVENTEEN YEAR OLD'S DERBY TRAM DASH

On 5th January 1952 seventeen-year-old Sheffield United youngster Graham Shaw turned up at Bramall Lane expecting to play for the reserves. He was stunned to learn instead that he had been selected for the first team at Hillsborough in the Steel City Derby.

Shaw was called up as a late replacement for full back Maurice McLaffery, who was not fit enough to play. He had to take a tram across the city and made it to Hillsboorugh shortly before the kick-off.

It was Shaw's full debut for United and there were 65,834 inside the ground. It was a hugely anticipated derby as Wednesday topped the table, but United were in fifth place just three points behind.

United won the game 3-1 with Alf Ringstead scoring twice and the other coming from George Hutchinson. Although Shaw had been outpaced in the build up to Wednesday's first half goal, he grew into the game as it went on and held his own against the opposition wingers.

Despite United completing a derby double, it would be Wednesday who celebrated promotion at the end of the season. Shaw went on to make over four hundred appearances for United and played five times for England.

1952
FACT 44
TEDDY DAVISON RESIGNS AFTER 20 YEARS

After two disappointing seasons, Teddy Davison resigned as Sheffield United manager in 1952. It brought a twenty-year association with the club to an end.

Davison spent eighteen years as a goalkeeper for Wednesday before becoming player-manager of Mansfield in 1926. A spell at Chesterfield followed before he was appointed as secretary-manager of United in 1932 following the death of John Nicholson.

Despite being relegated in Davison's second season in charge, the board stood by him and he made some astute signings. Jock Dodds came in on a free transfer and Jimmy Hagan cost just £2,500 in 1938. Davison led United, then in the Second Division, to the FA Cup final in 1936 although arguably the cup run cost his side promotion.

After promotion in 1939 national competition was suspended due to World War Two, but Davison remained in charge and led United to the Football League North title in 1946. He was unable to build on this though and after finishing sixth in 1947, United were relegated two years later.

United went agonisingly close to promotion in 1950, losing out to Wednesday by the finest of goal average margins. They failed to build on this and finished eighth in 1951 and then eleventh in 1952. Davison resigned from his position and returned to former club Chesterfield.

1953
SECOND
DIVISION CHAMPIONS

Three years after missing out by the faintest of margins, Sheffield United were promoted as champions in 1952-53.

Following two mid table finishes, Teddy Davison resigned and was replaced by Reg Freeman, who had led Rotherham to promotion from the Third Division North in 1950-51.

United had a mixed start, winning two and losing two of their first five games. Nearing the end of October they were third in the table, a point behind second place Leicester. However during November and December they won eight out of ten games and drew the other two. This opened up an eight point gap between them and third place.

United were consistent all season and never lost two successive matches. They were the division's top scorers with 97 goals and hit seven past both Leicester and Swansea at Bramall Lane.

Promotion was secured with two games to spare on 18th April when West Ham were beaten 3-1 at Bramall Lane. A week later they clinched the title with a 2-1 win over Fulham at Craven Cottage, finishing the season four points ahead of second place Huddersfield.

Sheffield United unveiled their floodlights at Bramall Lane on 16th March 1954, although this wasn't the first floodlit game at the ground.

At the time the lights were installed, the football authorities didn't allow competitive games to be played at night. United initially intended them to be used for training purposes only but decided to follow the lead of others and play some friendly matches.

The first game was a friendly against Rotherham, which attracted a crowd of around 17,000. United led 2-0 at the break but Rotherham refused to give up and pulled one back three minutes into the second half. The visitors continued to press but wasted two good chances and United held on for victory.

The following week, United met Scottish side Hibernian in a friendly. 30,000 fans witnessed an entertaining 3-3 draw, with five of the goals coming in the second half.

These weren't the first floodlit games at Bramall Lane however. 76 years beforehand, before United were even formed, the ground hosted a game advertised as being 'played by the aid of electric light' between a team of reds and blues. It was the first floodlit football match anywhere in the world.

1956
UNITED DOWN
WEDNESDAY UP

After three seasons in the First Division, Sheffield United were relegated in 1955-56, with Sheffield Wednesday coming up in their place.

Around Easter, United went four games unbeaten and looked likely to avoid the drop. With five games remaining they were three points clear of the relegation spaces, having played two games less than Aston Villa and Huddersfield who occupied them. However United then lost three in succession and sank to the bottom of the table.

Despite their position United still had one game in hand over those around them. On 28th April, the last full day of the season, they travelled to Tottenham who were still not mathematically safe. If United could avoid defeat, they would know exactly what they needed to do to stay up in their remaining game, at home to Wolves on 2nd May.

United got off to a great start, taking the lead on nine minutes. However they were dealt a huge blow after half an hour when Johnson got injured and couldn't continue. Tottenham equalised soon afterwards and scored two more in the second half to finish as 3-1 winners.

Results elsewhere meant United were down regardless of what happened against Wolves. There wouldn't even be a derby to look forward to, as Wednesday clinched promotion on the same day.

FACT 48
SHEFFIELD UNITED'S OLDEST PLAYER

The oldest player to represent Sheffield United was Jimmy Hagan, whose career at the club spanned twenty years.

Hagan joined United in 1938 from Derby County and scored ten goals in 28 appearances during his first season. United won promotion to Division One but football was suspended due to World War Two.

When competitive football resumed in 1946 Hagan, an inside forward, was appointed United's captain. Despite being relegated twice over the next ten years, he remained loyal to United and rejected opportunities to join First Division clubs. He was United's best player during this era with excellent ball control, dribbling, passing and shooting skills.

Hagan's last appearance for United was against former club Derby on 14th September 1957 at the age of 39 years and 256 days. The following March he was granted a testimonial game, which took place between a combined Sheffield XI and an International XI.

The board opted not to offer Hagan a coaching role, something they may well have regretted. He became manager at Peterborough, taking them into the Football League, then won the League Cup with West Bromwich Albion. Hagan then moved to Portugal where he won three successive league titles with Benfica.

1960
THE
LEAGUE CUP

FACT **49**

Sheffield United's first entry into the League Cup ended in disappointment when they were subjected to a shock defeat by Bury.

Along with most other Second Division teams, the Blades received a bye in the first round of the new competition. They were then drawn away against Bury of the Third Division.

The match took place at Bury's Gigg Lane ground on the evening of the 11th October. Jack Nibloe gave United the lead after just thirty seconds but midway through the first half Johnny Hubbard's drive levelled the score. After the break Bury scored twice, one of them a penalty, to complete a shock comeback in front of a crowd of 11,551. In the next round Bury were beaten 3-1 by Everton at Goodison Park.

Sheffield United fared better in the FA Cup that season, reaching the semi-final and also won promotion to the First Division. Bury were promoted too as champions of the Third Division. Nibloe, scorer of United's first League Cup goal left the club at the end of the season and was killed in a car crash in 1964.

PROMOTED WITH RECORD
WINNING SEQUENCE

Sheffield United were promoted back to the First Division in 1961. It was a season in which they won eleven home games in a row, an all-time club record.

Since relegation in 1956 United had finished seventh, sixth, third and then fourth. They started 1960-61 in a steady but not spectacular fashion, winning four and losing two of their first seven games.

A 1-0 win at Huddersfield on 14th September was the first of eight successive wins that took United to the top of the table, seven points clear of Norwich in third place. They won their opening eleven home games and didn't drop points at Bramall Lane until 3rd December, when they lost 3-2 to Bristol Rovers.

United were never out of the top two from their tenth game, a 3-2 win over Portsmouth. Promotion was clinched with two games to spare on 19th April 1961, when Derek Pace scored twice in a 3-1 win over Derby at Bramall Lane. They eventually finished in second place, six points ahead of Liverpool who were third.

If the last game of 1959-60 is included, United won twelve successive home league games. Whether the figure of eleven or twelve is quoted, it was a new club record which has not been equalled since.

1964
DEREK PACE
LEAVES

51

Derek Pace, who was Sheffield United's top scorer for seven successive seasons, left the club in 1964.

Pace scored after just eight minutes of his debut against Blackburn at Bramall Lane on Boxing Day 1957. His arrival coincided with an upturn in the team's form and he scored nine goals during eight successive victories in the Spring of 1958. Despite only joining in the middle of the season, he ended it as the United's top scorer.

In each of the next six seasons, Pace was United's leading scorer. In the promotion season of 1960-61 he found the net 26 times. He was consistent with both feet, his head and had the ability to score from half chances. Additionally he showed great sportsmanship and enthusiasm, making him a popular character on and off the pitch.

At the start of 1964-65 Pace suffered with an abdominal problem and lost his place to Mick Jones after three games. Unable to force his way back into the side, he joined Notts County in December 1964. His final goals tally for United was 140 goals in 253 appearances.

1966
JOE SHAW
RETIRES

FACT **52**

Joe Shaw, who made more appearances for Sheffield United than any other player, retired in 1966.

Shaw made his debut against Liverpool in August 1948 and became a regular in midfield the following season. In 1954 he began playing at centre half, where his lack of height didn't go against him. He had a remarkable ability to read the game and great powers of anticipation, allowing him to make interceptions and break up opposition play.

When Joe Mercer became manager he dropped Shaw, preferring a more physical presence. However he soon realised this was a mistake and Shaw came back even better. When United were promoted in 1961 Shaw was 33 years old, but he defied his years and captained them to a fifth place finish. Shaw finally retired in 1966, but not before he had a spell in the reserves nurturing younger players.

In 632 league appearances over eighteen seasons, Shaw scored only seven goals. He once went nine whole seasons without finding the net. He failed to score any of his 51 FA Cup appearances. In total he played 713 games for United in all competitions.

Shaw later managed York and Chesterfield. He died in 2007 and three years later a statue of him was unveiled at Bramall Lane.

1968
TOP
CAT

Tony Currie, nicknamed 'Top Cat' and voted Sheffield United's greatest ever player by fans, made his debut on 26th February 1968.

At the beginning of February United paid Watford £26,500 for midfielder Currie, an England youth international. He was just eighteen years and one month old but soon started to justify the fee. On his debut against Tottenham at Bramall Lane, he scored with a powerful header in the 45th minute to put United 2-1 up in a game they would eventually win 3-2.

United were relegated that year but Currie missed only seven games in the next three Division Two seasons, which culminated in promotion in 1971. He adapted to the First Division with ease and became one of the most exciting midfielders in the country. He scored ten times in 1971-72 and earned the first of his seventeen England caps.

Currie scored 54 goals in 313 league appearances for United, but when they were relegated again in 1976 his transfer request was accepted and he joined Leeds. In 2014, as part of United's 125th anniversary celebrations, he was voted the club's best ever player in a poll of supporters. The South Stand was renamed in his honour in 2018.

The nickname 'Top Cat' came from the American animated sitcom produced by Hanna-Barbera Productions. The central character, Top Cat was referred to as TC, the same initials as Currie's.

1968
FACT 54
ALAN WOODWARD'S DURABILITY

Sheffield United's leading post-war scorer is Alan Woodward, who had a remarkable record of being an ever present in five seasons out of seven.

Woodward made his debut in October 1964, a month after his eighteenth birthday. He developed a reputation as a strong and fast two-footed right winger, who was also a dead ball specialist.

In fourteen seasons Woodward scored 158 goals in 538 league appearances. Despite being relegated twice whilst at United, he remained loyal to the club despite opportunities to go elsewhere.

In 1968-69, Woodward began a remarkable run of consistency, which saw him miss just eleven games over ten seasons. In five of these seasons he appeared in all 42 league games, including the promotion campaign of 1970-71.

Despite playing on the wing, Woodward was United's top scorer on seven occasions. It was a travesty that he never played for England. He was the club's top scorer in 1977-78 but United fans were then dismayed when he announced that he would be moving to Tulsa Roughnecks in the Northern American Soccer League.

Woodward remains United's leading post war scorer and is third in the appearance stakes. He settled in Tulsa, where he died in 2015.

1971
FROM SECOND DIVISION TO TOP OF THE FIRST

1971 was a glorious year for Sheffield United as they won promotion back to the First Division. They then continued their form in the top flight and were top of the table at the end of September.

The Blades finished runners up in the Second Division, three points ahead of third placed Cardiff who they had beaten 5-1 at Bramall Lane in their penultimate fixture. During the summer they made just one major signing, paying £25,000 to Watford for Stewart Scullion.

Despite limited spending, United took the First Division by storm early on. Trevor Hockey was a rock in midfield and Tony Currie and Alan Woodward at their creative best. United won their first four fixtures, including a 1-0 at Arsenal, the previous season's Double winners to top the table.

United remained top throughout September when they remained unbeaten. After ten games, they were three points clear at the top, but the run finally came to an end when they lost 2-0 at second placed Manchester United in the first weekend of October.

The loss at Old Trafford was the start of four successive defeats for The Blades. However, they still finished a respectable tenth in the first season back in the top division.

1972
WATNEY CUP
FINALISTS

In 1972 Sheffield United were losing finalists in the short lived Watney Cup competition.

The summer competition was for the top two scoring sides in each of the four divisions that hadn't been promoted or qualified for Europe. United and Wolves were the First Division's representatives, with all the games taking place in the space of just eight days.

United started off with a 3-0 win at Third Division Notts County, before beating Fourth Division Peterborough 4-0 away from home in the semi-final. The final against Third Division Bristol Rovers was also at the opposition's ground, on Saturday 5th August.

Despite being two levels above their opponents, United struggled in the first half. They were glad to go into the break with the game still goalless, after three great saves by keeper Tom McAlister who was their best player by far.

The second half saw less action as both sides tired in the warm weather. After finishing 0-0, the game went straight to penalties. All ten players converted their kicks during the shoot-out, meaning it went to sudden death. Finally, with the fourteenth kick, Ted Hemsley's weak effort was easily saved by the Rovers keeper.

This was United's only participation during the four years, 1970 to 1973, that the Watney Cup took place.

1973
THE
SOUTH STAND

118 years of cricket at Bramall Lane came to an end in 1973 when work began on the new South Stand.

The ground was first opened for cricket in 1855, with football coming later. By the early 1960s football was clearly the main revenue earner, bringing in forty times the income of cricket. After winning promotion in 1971, the board decided to go it alone and gave the cricket club two years to vacate.

In August 1973 Yorkshire played Lancashire in the last County Championship match at Bramall Lane. The turf was cut up and sold for souvenirs and work began on the South Stand, which sat nearly 8,000 and doubled the ground's seating capacity.

Consisting of a single tier with a cantilevered roof meaning unobstructed views, it opened at the start of 1975-76. This turned out to be a disastrous one for United and ended in relegation, with many who were opposed to the end of first class cricket in Sheffield believing in Divine intervention.

The stand was given a radical overhaul in 2005, with new cladding and the wooden seats being replaced with plastic ones. In 2018 it was renamed the Tony Currie Stand. Despite Bramall Lane's modern look, it is now the oldest stadium in the world currently hosting professional football.

1976
SHEFFIELD UNITED'S
WORST SEASON

FACT **58**

The worst ever season statistically was in 1975-76 when they were relegated from the First Division. They collected their lowest ever points total of 22 and lost 26 of their 42 games.

United had finished sixth in 1974-75, missing out on European qualification by just one point. However the money spent on the new stand meant there was little left for new players.

After drawing 1-1 with Derby at Bramall Lane on the opening day, United lost their next seven games. They beat fellow strugglers Burnley in their ninth game but then lost two more in succession. This led to the dismissal of manager Ken Furphy, who was replaced by Jimmy Sirrel.

Sirrel couldn't stop the slide and his first victory was a 2-1 home win over Aston Villa on 14th February, his seventeenth match in charge.

Relegation was confirmed on the final Saturday in March, when United lost 5-0 at Tottenham. Their form suddenly improved, winning four, drawing one and losing one of their last six games. Despite this they still ended the season with less goals scored and more coceded than anyone else. Their final points tally of 22 is an all time club record low.

1976
FACT 59
UNITED'S YOUNGEST LEAGUE SCORER

A rare bright spot during the dreadful 1975-76 season was the emergence of Simon Stainrod, who became the club's youngest league scorer.

The teenage striker made his debut in the 5-0 defeat at Tottenham that confirmed United's relegation. The following week against Norwich at Carrow Road he scored in a 3-1 victory, United's first on the road that season. He was aged just 17 years and 61 days.

A week later in his first appearance at Bramall Lane, Stainrod scored the winning goal in a 3-2 victory over West Ham. It was no more than he deserved after twice going close in the first half and he played in the four remaining fixtures that season.

Over the next two seasons, Stainrod scored nine goals in 45 Second Division appearances as he developed a good partnership with Keith Edwards. In March 1979 with the club in need of funds, he was sold to Oldham for £60,000.

Stainrod enjoyed a varied career over twenty years with eleven clubs in England, Scotland and France. After managing in Scotland in the 1990s, he moved to France and is now a FIFA licensed agent.

Sheffield United did not have a crest containing blades until 1977, when it was introduced by manager Jimmy Sirrel.

United only began wearing a crest on their shirts in 1965, using the city's coat of arms. However the club faced problems regarding this when it was copyrighted by the city council.

In 1977 Sirrel introduced a new crest featuring blades. Sirrel is generally credited for designing the crest, but it is also claimed that former player Jimmy Hagan had drawn it twenty years earlier.

The crest consisted of two crossed blades in the form of swords, with a white rose to represent Yorkshire. The background was black and there was a red circle to incorporate the club colours. The words 'Sheffield United' were added, as was 1889, the year of foundation.

Sirrel was not around much longer after the crest was introduced. With United struggling at the wrong end of the Second Division he left on 27th September 1977. Two weeks later he took over at Notts County, who like the Blades were battling relegation. Both clubs went on to avoid the drop that season.

Between 1987 and 1999 the crest design altered slightly but in 2000 it went back to the original style.

1978
SABELLA
FACT 61 INSTEAD OF MARADONA

When Sheffield United's manager Harry Haslam travelled to Argentina in the summer of 1978, he felt the price for Diego Maradona was too high and signed Alex Sabella instead.

Maradona, who would become one of the world's best ever players, was then an unproven seventeen-year-old. Haslam baulked at the asking price of over half a million pounds demanded by Argentinos Juniors, but did agree to pay River Plate £160,000 for twenty-three-year-old midfielder Alex Sabella.

There was no doubt Sabella had outstanding talent although he did lack pace. His control, dribbling, vision and passing were outstanding. Too often his teammates simply weren't able to keep up with his talents and his visionary play was wasted. United were relegated that season but Sabella chose to stay and await a bid from a top flight club rather than be transferred to Second Division Sunderland.

In the summer of 1980, after eight goals in 76 United appearances, Sabella was sold to Leeds for £400,000. However he returned to Argentina after just one season. He went on to manage the Argentine national side and led them to the 2014 World Cup final, losing 1-0 to Germany.

1978

FACT 62 FACING THE CHAMPIONS OF TWO CONTINENTS

In the space of just three days in 1978, Sheffield United welcomed both the European and South American champions to Bramall Lane.

In the second round of the League Cup, the Blades were drawn at home to Liverpool, winners of the European Cup for the previous two seasons.

On 28th August 35,000 fans packed into Bramall Lane. Liverpool's starting line-up included nine players who had faced Bruges in the European Cup final three months earlier. For eighty minutes United did nothing but defend and could easily have been behind by double figures. In one hectic five-minute spell the ball was twice cleared off the line and keeper Steve Conroy made three saves.

With ten minutes remaining United had a rare attack and teenager Gary Hamson's drive from the edge of the area beat Reds keeper Ray Clemence. United held on for a famous victory over a side who won the league title at a canter that season.

Just two nights later, as part of the deal that brought Alex Sabella to the club, United hosted River Plate, holders of the Copa America. This time the crowd was 22,000 and the South American champions, who included Argentina's World Cup winning captain Daniel Passarella, won 2-1.

The Blades were relegated to the third tier of English football for the first time in 1979.

After finishing eleventh in their first season back in the Second Division, United were in the relegation zone when they parted company with manager Jimmy Sirrel at the end of September 1977. Under caretaker manager Cec Coldwell and then Harry Haslam they eventually finished in twelfth in 1977-78.

During 1978-79 United struggled to get any form of consistency going. Scoring goals was not a problem and they ended the season with one more than champions Crystal Palace, it was just that the defence shipped them too easily.

United didn't actually enter the bottom three until the end of April, when they lost 6-2 at Sunderland. They won one of their next three games, meaning only a three goal victory in their final fixture against Leicester at Bramall Lane would save them.

On the evening of 8th May United could only draw 2-2 in a game marred by a pitch invasion by hundreds of fans, during which Leicester's Alan Lee was kneed in the back. It meant United would be playing outside of the top two divisions for the first time since joining the Football League in 1892.

1981
PENALTY DRAMA
MEANS RELEGATION

The Blades were relegated to the Fourth Division on the final day of the 1980-81 season after a dramatic last five minutes at Bramall Lane.

The season started promisingly for United, who won their opening three league fixtures. By mid October though, they had fallen into the bottom half of the table after a dreadful return of just one point from the last six games.

United rallied briefly and heading into the Christmas holiday they were in eighth place, only to have a terrible second half of the season. They were already on a downward slope when manager Harry Haslam was forced to retire through ill health in January. He was replaced by player coach Martin Peters, who failed to turn things around.

It meant that United needed a point in their final game of the season, at home to Walsall, to avoid relegation. Defeat would mean Walsall stayed up at United's expense.

With five minutes remaining, Walsall took the lead from the penalty spot. United were then given a lifeline in the last minute when a penalty was awarded for handball. To the horror of Blades fans, Don Givens' effort was weak and easily saved. Just six years after almost qualifying for Europe, United were in the Fourth Division.

1982
DIVISION FOUR
CHAMPIONS

FACT **65**

After the heartbreak of relegation, Sheffield United went straight back up in style, finishing the 1981-82 season as Fourth Division champions.

United secured something of a managerial coup by appointing Ian Porterfield. He had just led Rotherham to promotion from the Third Division but agreed to drop two levels.

The season started unspectacularly, with United occupying sixth place at the end of September. However, they then went on a four month unbeaten run in the league, lifting them up to second at the end of January.

Throughout the season Bob Hatton and Keith Edwards were prolific in attack. The latter scored 35 goals to be the top scorer across all four divisions. There were some big wins, with United scoring four or more goals on eight occasions, including a 7-3 thrashing of Northampton at Bramall Lane.

After losing at Scunthorpe on 20th February, United went the rest of the season unbeaten. Promotion was secured in the final home game on 8th May, with a 4-0 win over fellow hopefuls Peterborough in front of 23,932 fans. The following week United won 2-0 at Darlington to secure the title and end the season with just four defeats in 46 games.

FACT 66
A NAIL-BITING PROMOTION

Promotion from the Third Division was secured by the finest of margins in 1983-84, finishing above fourth placed Hull city on goals scored.

United were unbeaten in their first seven games and second in the table at Christmas. Promotion was in their own hands with three games left but a home defeat to rivals Wimbledon left it extremely tight.

United were vying with Hull for the final promotion place. They were a point ahead, but Hull had a game in hand which would be played after United had completed their fixtures.

On the last day of the regular season United beat Newport 2-0 at Bramall Lane, while Hull could only draw 0-0 at home to Bristol Rovers. This meant that Hull needed to win by three goals at Burnley in their final game to go up.

On 15th May a few hundred United fans travelled to Turf Moor to cheer Burnley on. Others listened to score updates every quarter of an hour on Radio Sheffield, while some managed to pick up live commentary on Radio Humberside.

With twenty minutes remaining it was tense as Hull led 2-0. They couldn't get that one more goal though so with the same points and goal difference, United went up courtesy of scoring 86 goals to Hull's 71.

1986
FACT 67 KEITH EDWARDS LEAVES FOR A SECOND TIME

One of the club's most prolific post-war scorers was Keith Edwards, who scored 171 goals in two separate spells.

Edwards was eighteen when he made his debut against Leicester in an FA Cup third round tie in January 1976. That season ended in relegation to the Second Division and in 1976-77 he finished as the club's leading scorer.

In 1978 Edwards was sold to Hull City for £50,000 and he was leading scorer there for three successive seasons. When both Hull and The Blades were relegated to the Fourth Division in 1981, manager Ian Porterfield paid £100,000 to bring Edwards back to Bramall Lane. He scored 35 times as United were promoted as champions in their first season at that level.

When United were promoted in 1983-84 he was leading scorer again, this time with 34 goals. He continued to perform at the higher level, topping the club scoring charts again in the next two seasons.

Edwards left the club in August 1986 when a £125,000 fee was agreed with Leeds. His final goals tally for United was 171 in all competitions. He is in both first and second positions for most goals in a season for the club since World War Two and played for the Blades in all four divisions.

1988
DAVE
BASSETT

In January 1988 Dave Bassett was appointed as manager of Sheffield United. It was the beginning of a memorable period of just under eight years in charge, which saw two relegations and two promotions.

Bassett had gained his managerial reputation by taking Wimbledon from the Fourth to First Division in the space of just four seasons. Feeling he had taken the club as far as he could, he left in 1987 for Watford, but was sacked after just eight months with the club bottom of the First Division.

Bassett was unable to prevent United's slide into the Third Division, but after bringing in his own backroom team they came straight back up. There was then a second successive promotion as top flight football returned to Bramall Lane for the first time in sixteen years.

The Blades finished thirteenth, ninth and fourteenth in their first three seasons in the top flight, which became the Premier League in 1992. However in 1993-94 they were relegated in the last few minutes of the season. Bassett was unable to mount a promotion challenge and United finished eighth in what was now the First Division. He resigned in December 1995 with the club nearer the bottom than the top.

1988

FACT 69 RELEGATION VIA
THE PLAY-OFFS

Although Dave Bassett had great success with Sheffield United, he had to go backwards before going forwards. At the end of 1987-88 United faced the agony of being relegated from the Second Division following a play-off defeat.

Promotion/relegation play-offs were introduced by the Football League in 1986-87. The following season United finished third from bottom of the table, which would previously have meant automatic relegation. This time they had a chance to retain their status at that level if they could win two ties against Third Division opposition.

In the first leg of their semi-final on 15th May, United lost 1-0 against Bristol City at Ashton Gate. Three days later at Bramall Lane, City took a first half lead, leaving United with an uphill task in the second period. Colin Morris made it 1-1 after 49 minutes, but United were unable to find a winner and were relegated.

This would be the last year that sides could be relegated via the play-offs. From 1989 they would be used to determine promotion only. Although that year United did go up automatically, they have had plenty more involvement since.

1989
PROMOTED IN
CENTENARY YEAR

United had a memorable centenary season in 1988-89. Dave Bassett led them straight back up with a second place finish and automatic promotion.

Five wins out of their opening six games meant United were top of the table at the end of September. By Christmas they were third, but only two points behind Port Vale having lost just once at Bramall Lane.

A run of ten games unbeaten between January and March kept up the pressure and opened up a big gap on fourth place. Wolves looked assured of finishing top, with United and Vale vying for the second automatic spot.

By the end of April promotion was in United's hands. On 6th May, they hammered Swansea 5-1 in their final home game of the season. They now needed just two points from their last two away games to guarantee promotion but one would almost certainly be enough due to their superior goal difference. The form of astute signings Brian Deane and Tony Agana were key to this, with both finding the net twenty times.

Promotion was as good as sealed with a 2-2 draw at champions Wolves on 9th May. Despite losing 2-0 at Bristol City four days later, United were still promoted due to Vale's failure to win by eleven goals at Fulham.

A second successive promotion was secured on the last day of 1989-90, winning 5-2 at Leicester to ensure First Division football was back at Bramall Lane after fourteen years.

The Blades lost just one of their first eighteen games. By the halfway stage at Christmas they were in second place, six ahead of Sunderland. During the Spring however their form dipped slightly, which coupled with a late surge by Newcastle meant the promotion race went right down to the wire.

Going into the final day of the season United were on 82 points along with Leeds, who were ahead on goal difference. Newcatle were two points behind and with just the top two going up automatically, one of the three was destined for the play-offs.

All three candidates were away from home in their last game. The Blades were at mid table Leicester while Leeds and Newcaslte were at Bournemouth and Midlesbrough respectively, both of whom were battling relegation.

United fell behind to an early goal but struck back to lead 4-1 at half-time. The game finished 5-2 and afterwards thousands of jubilant fans invaded the pitch, where manager Dave Bassett was stripped to his underpants. Within the space of fourteen eventful years, United had gone from the First to Fourth Division and back.

1991
A
GREAT ESCAPE

FACT **72**

After looking certainties for relegation at Christmas, a remarkable turnaround was produced to avoid going straight back down to the Second Division.

The Blades failed to win any of their first sixteen games, leaving them rock bottom and ten points from safety. They finally tasted victory on 22nd December when Nottingham Forest were beaten 3-2 at Bramall Lane. United then won 1-0 at Luton, narrowing the gap to five points. With only two teams going down that season, there was suddenly hope.

On New Year's Day, United beat second bottom QPR 1-0, meaning they were just four points behind the Londoners with a game in hand. Two defeats followed but United then went on a run of seven straight wins, starting with a 1-0 defeat of Derby on 26th January. The winning sequence included a vital 1-0 win at struggling Sunderland and by the end of March the Blades were in twelfth, six points above the bottom two.

Survival was ensured on 20th April with a 2-2 draw at home to Tottenham who had hammered United 4-0 in the earlier fixture at White Hart Lane. The Blades had completed a great escape with three matches to spare

FACT 73

1992
THE
PREMIER LEAGUE

In 1992-93 Sheffield United competed in the inaugural Premier League season.

Television revenues were the key factor behind the creation of the Premier League, meaning income would be split between the twenty top flight clubs rather than across all four divisions.

The Blades' first game under the new format was at home to Manchester United. Brian Deane headed their first goal of the new era after just five minutes. He made it 2-0 from the penalty spot early in the second half after Alan Cork was bundled over in the area. The visitors pulled a goal back but the Blades held on for victory.

After the opening day victory United then picked up just one point from six games. They eventually finished thirteenth, with Deane the club's leading scorer on fourteen goals.

Other highlights of the season at Bramall Lane were a 6-0 win over Tottenham, beating Liverpool 1-0 and victory over champions Leeds. Dave Bassett was awarded the Manager of the Year by the League Managers Association, on the basis of having done the best job with the resources available.

1993
STEEL CITY
SEMI-FINAL

In the semi-finals of the 1992-93 FA Cup, both Sheffield clubs faced each other at Wembley, but sadly it was Wednesday who came out triumphant.

This was United's first FA Cup semi-final since 1961 and the game with Wednesday was initially scheduled to take place at Elland Road in Leeds. However with the other semi-final between Arsenal and Tottenham taking place at Wembley, United and Wednesday successfully lobbied for their game to take place there as well.

The Blades had the worst possible start when they conceded a free kick in a dangerous position after a minute. Chris Waddle's curler gave keeper Alan Kelly no chance. Waddle ran United's defence ragged and there was a let off when Paul Warhurst's shot hit the bar. Then against the run of play Franz Carr set up Alan Cork to equalise a minute before half-time.

The second half was mainly Wednesday but Kelly was equal to everything. The match went into extra time and two minutes into the second period Mark Bright headed in from a corner. United couldn't find a way back into the game and it was Wednesday who would be returning to Wembley for the final.

1994
RELEGATED IN
INJURY TIME

In an astonishing final twist Sheffield United were relegated from the Premier League in the last seconds of the 1993-94 season.

With little money for new signings, United struggled for most of the campaign. Although tight at the back, they also had one of the worst attacks in the Premier League. They failed to adequately replace the departed Brian Deane and leading scorer Jostein Flo managed just nine goals.

Going into the final stretch things looked bleak for United, but four wins from six lifted them out of the bottom three. On the final day of the season, United were one of six teams fighting to avoid going down with already relegated Swindon.

United started the day fifth from bottom, ahead of Ipswich on goal difference and one point above Everton. They were away to Chelsea, but led 1-0 at the break as Everton were losing to Wimbledon.

Although Chelsea equalised, Glyn Hodges restored United's lead with half an hour to go. Mark Stein made it 2-2 with fifteen minutes remaining but if all scores remained the same The Blades would still stay up.

Even though Everton came back to lead Wimbledon, United still looked safe at the expense of Ipswich who were also drawing. However in injury time Stein added another and United were down.

FACT 76

1994
ANGLO
ITALIAN CUP

A brief foray was made onto the Continent in 1994-95 when The Blades were one of eight English entrants in the much maligned Anglo-Italian Cup.

The competition was for second tier sides from England and Italy. United were in a group of eight teams, consisting of four from each country. They had to play four games, all against Italian sides, two at home and two away. The incentive for those taking part was the prospect of a final at Wembley.

United began with a 2-1 home defeat to Udinese. They then drew 2-2 with Piacenza in Italy before drawing 3-3 draw with Ancona at Bramall Lane in front of just 1,827 fans. Their final game was a 4-1 win at Cesena but this was not enough to finish as the best placed English side and they were eliminated.

It was the first and only ever time United appeared in the competition, which had been relatively popular in the 1970s but marred by violence on occasions. When it was briefly revived in the 1990s for four seasons, United were in the Premier League for two of them and didn't compete in the final tournament, 1995-96.

1996
WHEN
SATURDAY COMES

In 1996 Bramall Lane featured on the cinema screens, courtesy of the Maria Giese directed film *When Saturday Comes*.

The plot centres around 25 year old brewery worker Jimmy Muir (played by Sean Bean) who plays amateur football locally. He is offered a trial by United but blows his chance when he gets drunk the night before. Muir then loses his job and his girlfriend and suffers the death of his brother in a mining accident.

Muir re-evaluates his life and he becomes determined to succeed as a footballer. He does so but has to overcome prejudices of experiences teammates who feel he does not belong there. His acceptance comes in spectacular style though as he scores a hat-trick in a 3-2 victory over Manchester United.

Amongst the cast was United legend Tony Currie, playing himself. Some of the scenes for the film were shot at Bramall Lane at half-time during a match with Manchester United, with Bean taking a penalty. Others used a crowd of about 3,000 extras, who moved around the ground for different shots to make it appear full.

The film was released in February 1996, with six screens set aside at Meadowhall on opening night. It was also aired at the Cannes Film Festival.

Sheffield United missed out on promotion to the Premier League in agonising circumstances in 1996-97. As the play-off final looked set to go to extra time they were denied promotion by a last-minute winner.

The Blades finished the regular season in fifth place then beat Ipswich on away goals to set up a final with Crystal Palace at Wembley on 26th May.

After getting the better of the opening stages, Palace settled and had more of the play for the rest of the first half. The Blades then suffered a blow when Don Hutchison was forced off shortly before the break with a broken collarbone.

In the second half United performed better and the for the first twenty minutes enjoyed their best spell of the game, with Jan Age Fjortoft dangerous at set pieces. The Norwegian striker had their best chance of the half, firing just wide of the post.

With a minute remaining United had to defend a corner. Carl Tiler thought he had cleared the danger but David Hopkin picked up the loose ball outside the area and curled a shot past Simon Tracey into the net. The Blades lost out to virtually the last kick of the game.

1999
FA CUP
REMATCH

When United were beaten in controversial circumstances by Arsenal in the fifth round of the FA Cup in 1998-99, they were sensationally offered a rematch.

With fourteen minutes remaining and the scores level at 1-1, United keeper Alan Kelly kicked the ball out of play so that Lee Morris could be treated for an injury. However when play resumed Kanu intercepted a throw that was meant for a United player, setting up Marc Overmars to score.

There were furious protests at the unfairness, with play not resuming for eight minutes. As no rule had been broken the referee had no option but to let the goal stand. Afterwards Arsene Wenger, when asked his opinion said: "The second goal is a controversial goal and we feel that it is not right. We have the feeling that we didn't win the game like we want to win our games."

Wenger's offer to replay the game was accepted by United and the FA agreed to the request. Ten days later the teams met again but United were unable to take their second chance. They again lost 2-1 but this time the circumstances of the result were not disputed.

In 1999 Sheffield born Neil Warnock, a manager renowned as a promotion specialist, was appointed as Blades' boss, the beginning of a seven and a half year tenure at the club.

A journeyman player with non-league and lower division clubs, Warnock's first notable achievement as a manager was winning promotion to the Football League with Scarborough in 1987. He then won four promotions via the play-offs in the 1990s, including taking Notts County from the Third to First Division.

Warnock took United to two semi-finals in 2003 then lost his first play-off final. In 2006 he took United up to the Premier League but resigned three days after the end of the 2006-07 season, when The Blades were relegated.

Chairman Kevin McCabe was full of praise for Warnock after he announced his decision to quit, saying "Neil is a great motivational team manager and he has played a key role in assisting the reshaping of the club. We have come a long way with Neil and, on a personal note, I thank him for his commitment to United. He is and always will be a Blade and has a special place here at Bramall Lane."

2002
THE BATTLE OF
BRAMALL LANE

The infamous Battle of Bramall Lane in 2002 saw Sheffield United's game with West Bromwich Albion abandoned as the Blades had only six players left on the pitch.

After just nine minutes United were reduced to ten men when Simon Tracy was sent off for handling outside of the area. Reserve keeper Wilko de Vogt came off the bench in place of Peter Ndlovu and at half-time Albion led 1-0.

United fell further behind after 62 minutes and three minutes later had substitute George Santos red carded for a bad foul on Andy Johnson. In the fracas that followed, another United substitute Patrick Suffo was dismissed for an attempted head butt.

The Blades were now down to eight players so it was no surprise when Albion went 3-0 up in the 77th minute. Two minutes later Michael Brown had to limp off with injury, reducing United to seven men.

With eight minutes to go, Robert Ullathorne had to go off injured. This led to the referee, abandoning the game in line with guidance that teams should not continue playing with just six players.

Rather than order a replay, the Football League awarded Albion a 3-0 victory and United were fined £10,000. Santos and Suffo never played for the club again.

2003
TWO
SEMI-FINALS

The semi-finals of both domestic cups were reached during 2002-03 but were beaten by Premier League opposition in each of them.

In the League Cup The Blades were drawn at home in every round. They overcame York and Wycombe, then Premier League Leeds and Sunderland to reach the quarter finals, where fellow Championship side Crystal Palace were beaten.

In the semi-final United were drawn against Liverpool and came from behind to win the first leg 2-1 at Bramall Lane. At Anfield, Liverpool took an early lead but United held on for extra-time. Eventually Michael Owen's 107th minute goal settled the tie.

United also had home ties in every round of the FA Cup. After beating Cheltenham, Ipswich and Walsall, they knocked Premier League Leeds out of a cup for the second time that season.

The semi-final was against Arsenal at Old Trafford. The Blades were furious when the referee didn't stop play for an injury in the build-up to Freddie Ljundberg's goal. Towards the end of the game Paul Peschisolido looked certain to score with a header but goalkeeper David Seaman made an incredible one handed save.

Manager Neil Warnock was fuming afterwards, saying "The manner in which we have lost this match is an absolute disgrace". Both Liverpool and Arsenal went on to win their respective finals.

2003
ECSTACY AND AGONY
IN PLAY-OFFS

After the agony of losing two cup semi-finals in 2002-03, Sheffield United missed out on promotion to the Premier League. Despite winning a thrilling semi-final second leg against Nottingham Forest at Bramall Lane, they were well beaten in the final.

The Blades finished third in the Championship, twelve points behind second placed Leicester. In the first leg of their play-off semi-final at the City Ground, Michael Brown's penalty earned them a 1-1 draw.

In the second leg, Forest led 1-0 at half-time and extended their lead in the 58th minute. Brown scored two minutes later to give United hope and Steve Kabba made it 2-2 with 68 minutes gone.

Away goals didn't count double so the tie went to extra time. Shortly before the end of the first period Paul Pechisolido gave United the lead with a brilliant solo effort. With three minutes remaining it was 4-2 thanks to a Des Walker own goal but Robert Page also turned into his own net to ensure a tense finish. Afterwards boss Neil Warnock told the media "I don't think my lads know when they are beaten".

Sadly the final against Wolves at the Millennium Stadium in Cardiff was forgettable. United were 3-0 down at half-time and missed a chance to fight their way back when Brown had a 48th minute penalty saved.

When Alan Quinn scored the only goal of the game in Sheffield United's win over Sheffield Wednesday on 3rd December 2005, he became the first player to score for both clubs in the Steel City Derby.

Irishman Quinn was released by Wednesday in the summer of 2004, following their failure to win promotion from the third tier. Neil Warnock snapped him up on a free transfer and during 2004-05 he scored seven goals in 43 Championship appearances.

Preparations for the first league derby in three seasons were disrupted by Premier League Portsmouth's attempts to lure Warnock to the South Coast. However he rejected the offer and decided to remain at Bramall Lane.

United should have taken an early lead but Steve Kabba miss-kicked from just three yards. When they did go ahead in the 24th minute Quinn's shot appeared to hit Shipperley before going over the line, but the former Wednesday player was credited with the goal. Wednesday never looked like getting back into the game, their one shot on target being a free kick.

Quinn was now forgiven for the goal he scored in Wednesday's 3-1 win over united at Bramall Lane in 2002-03. He remained at United until January 2008 when he joined Ipswich. No other player has equalled his feat of scoring for both clubs in the Steel City Derby.

United expanded into Asia in 2006 with the purchase and rebranding of a Chinese second tier side.

The purchase of Chengu Wuniu was part of a strategy to build partnerships with clubs abroad where players could be developed. United also bought controlling interests in clubs in Hungary and Australia, but it was the Chinese investment that attracted the most interest.

Rebranded as Chengdu Blades, the Chinese club had their shirts changed to red and white stripes and a new logo with crossed swords. Two of the biggest names in Chinese football, Lie Tie and Sun Jihai, who both had Premier League experience, were transferred to Chengdu.

Replica shirts were sold at Bramall Lane and the Chengdu players received a great reception when they visited the city.

Chengdu Blades were promoted in 2007 and improved in each of the next three seasons in the Chinese Super League. However following a match fixing scandal in 2010 they were demoted back to the second tier.

With United now struggling at the wrong end of the Championship, foreign investment was far from a priority and the partnership dissolved.

2006
PROMOTED TO
THE PREMIER LEAGUE

After two play-off final defeats since their relegation in 1994, promotion to the Premier League was won in style in 2005-06.

The Blades won ten of their first eleven games. Along with Reading they opened up a big gap at the top and at the turn of the year United were second in the table. They were seven points behind Reading but eleven ahead of Leeds.

A key to United's success over the season was not being reliant on one striker to score the goals. They scored 76 over the season, the third highest in the division, but they were spread around the team and leading scorer Ade Akinbiyi netted only fifteen of these.

Neil Warnock's side secured promotion with three games to spare thanks to a 1-0 win at Cardiff on 14th April. It meant there was a carnival atmosphere on the final day of the season when the Blades won 1-0 at home against Crystal Palace. They also celebrated with an open-top bus tour from Bramall Lane to the Town Hall with tens of thousands lining the route.

United finished the season with an impressive 92 points, eleven clear of Watford in third.

2007
RELEGATED BY
AN INELIGIBLE PLAYER

When the club was relegated on the last day of the 2006-07 season, there was anger that the player whose goal sent them down turned out to be ineligible.

United started the day in sixteenth place and were at home to Wigan, who were three points below in the last relegation spot. A point would be enough for United and even if they lost West Ham, who were level on points but with an inferior goal difference, were not expected to get a result at champions Manchester United.

United's world fell apart just before half-time. Drawing 1-1, they conceded a penalty which was dispatched by former Blades player David Unsworth. Over at Old Trafford, Carlos Tevez put West Ham ahead against a Manchester United side who had a number of star names left on the bench.

There was no further scoring in either game and The Blades were relegated as Wigan had the better goal difference. Neil Warnock was critical of Sir Alex Ferguson's team selection for Manchester United who were playing in the following week's FA Cup final.

It later transpired that Tevez was part owned by a third party, against Premier League rules. Rather than face a points deduction, West Ham were fined instead. They were later ordered to pay £20 million in compensation to The Blades.

2008
DEATH OF
DEREK DOOLEY

FACT **88**

Derek Dooley, uniquely revered by fans of Sheffield's two professional clubs, died in 2008.

The son of a steelworker, Dooley was a prolific goalscorer for Sheffield Wednesday in the early 1950s. In an accidental collision with a goalkeeper, he suffered a horrific injury that required the amputation of his right leg.

Dooley had scouting and coaching roles with Wednesday, as well as running the club's lottery before becoming manager in 1971. He was sacked two years later and vowed never to return to Hillsborough.

In 1974 Dooley agreed to become Sheffield United's commercial manager. He remained with the club in various administrative roles, rising to chief executive before retiring in 1996. By now he had settled his differences with Wednesday and was applauded by both sets of fans when he attended a derby at Hillsborough in 1992.

With United £4 million in debt, Dooley agreed to return to the club as chairman in 1999. He oversaw a turnaround that led to the Blades returning to the top flight in 2006, when he stepped down to become a life vice president.

Dooley died aged 78 in 2008. Thousands of fans from United and Wednesday stood outside Sheffield Cathedral for his funeral service. United's academy was renamed in his honour and two years later a statue of him was unveiled at Bramall Lane.

2009
TEN MAN BLADES
89 LOSE PLAY-OFF FINAL

The 2009 Championship play-off final was lost in frustrating circumstances. Although Burnley's winning goal was worthy of any Wembley occasion, United manager Kevin Blackwell was furious at some of referee Mike Dean's decisions.

The Blades finished third in the league, three points behind Birmingham who went up automatically. They then beat Preston in the semi-final, drawing 1-1 away then winning 1-0 at Bramall Lane.

In the first half of the final against Burnley, United were disappointing in the first half and failed to create a meaningful chance. Burnley took the lead in the thirteenth minute when Wade Elliot drove the ball into the top corner of the net from outside the area.

Too often the Blades resorted to long balls and they were fortunate to stay in the game after 55 minutes, when Nick Montgomery blocked a goalbound effort on the line.

United were denied penalty appeals by Dean in each half. The first was open to debate but replays showed the second was definitely a foul. Substitute Jamie Ward was sent off with eleven minutes left for a second yellow card, both of them for handball.

During the last ten minutes United offered little and Burnley comfortably held on. To compound United's misery, Lee Hendrie was red carded after the final whistle for abusive language towards Dean.

2011
FOUR MANAGERS
AND RELEGATION

A turbulent season in 2010-11 saw four managers and relegation to the third tier of English football for the first time in 23 years.

Kevin Blackwell, who had led the Blades to the play-off final in 2009, left by mutual consent after the second league game, a 3-0 home defeat to QPR. He was replaced by Gary Speed, the Welshman's first managerial appointment.

MANAGERS
THIS WAY
←

When Speed left in December to become manager of Wales, United were a point above the relegation zone. First team coach John Carver took over on a caretaker basis, winning one and drawing two before Micky Adams was appointed just before the New Year.

Adams got off to a disastrous start and failed to win any of his first twelve games in charge. When they finally beat Nottingham Forest on 8th March, they were second bottom and six points adrift of safety.

Four successive defeats in April left United on the brink, but two wins in a row did give them an outside chance with two games remaining. However a 2-2 home draw with Barnsley in the penultimate game of the season confirmed their demotion to League One.

2012
PLAY-OFF FINAL DEFEAT
CREATES RECORD

FACT **91**

An unwanted record was gained in the 2012 League One play-offs. Their penalty shootout defeat was their fourth play-off final loss, more than any other club.

The Blades finished third in the table, three points behind Wednesday who were in the second automatic promotion spot. In the semi-final they finally overcame Stevenage in the 85th minute of the second leg at Bramall Lane, when Christopher Porter scored the first and only goal of the tie.

On a baking hot day at Wembley, United and opponents Huddersfield took several water breaks during the game. There were few chances for either side, but Huddersfield did hit the bar twice. United were twice denied late in normal time by the keeper and it was 0-0 after ninety minutes.

Thirty minutes of extra time couldn't separate the sides and the game went to penalties. After four kicks each it was just 1-1, but each side then converted all of their next six efforts. This meant that the goalkeepers had to take their turn, with Huddersfield's Alex Smithies scoring but United's Steve Simonsen blazing over the bar.

The defeat was United's fourth in a play-off final, a record they share with Brentford.

The youngest player to represent the club in a league game is Louis Reed. He was just 16 years and 257 days old when he made his debut against Rotherham on 8th April 2014.

A product of United's Academy, Reed got his chance as manager Nigel Clough made changes ahead of a forthcoming FA Cup semi-final. United had little chance of reaching the League One play offs, meaning Reed was given a place on the bench.

With sixteen minutes remaining and the score still 0-0, Reed was given his opportunity and replaced Jose Baxter. The young midfielder ended up on the winning side as a late penalty converted by Ben Davies earned United victory.

That summer Reed was given a professional contract and started the first league game of 2014-15, a season in which he made 32 appearances in all competitions. In 2015-16 he played 25 times, but didn't feature at all in the league during the following campaign which ended in promotion.

Reed spent 2017-18 on loan with Chesterfield, scoring four goals from 42 appearances in League Two. He then joined Peterborough for an undisclosed fee.

2014
FA CUP
GIANT KILLERS

The "93" with "FACT" vertical on left.

Despite missing out on the League One play-offs in 2013-14, Sheffield United enjoyed a giant killing FA Cup run that took them to the semi-finals.

The Blades made it through to the third round with away wins over Colchester and Cambridge. They were then drawn away to Premier League Aston Villa, where Ryan Flynn's goal ten minutes from time gave them a 2-1 win.

In the fourth round United were paired with another Premier League side, Fulham, at home. After a 1-1 draw at Bramall Lane the replay at Craven Cottage looked likely to go to penalties, but Shaun Miller struck a last gasp winner at the end of extra time.

United were the lowest ranked team left in the fifth round draw, where they were drawn at home to Nottingham Forest of the Championship. After trailing 1-0 at half-time, Conor Coady equalised midway through the second period and two goals in the last minute from Christopher Porter took the Blades through to the quarter finals.

Another Championship side, Charlton, were beaten 2-0 at Bramall Lane as United became the first third tier semi-finalists since Wycombe in 2001. Sadly for United the semi-final against Hull City at Wembley was a step too far. Despite leading 2-1 at the break, they ended up losing 5-3.

FACT 94
THE HIGHEST SCORING PLAY-OFF

Sheffield United were involved in both, the highest ever scoring individual Football League play-off game, and tie at the end of 2014-15.

After finishing fifth in League One, United faced Swindon over two legs in the play-off semi-final. In the first leg at Bramall Lane on 7th May, United led 1-0 at half-time but ended up losing 2-1. Agonisingly, Swindon's winner came in the fourth minute of added time.

At the County Ground on 11th May, United were left with a mountain to climb after falling three behind in just eighteen minutes. By half-time though they had pulled it back to 3-2 on the night, 5-3 on aggregate.

Any hopes of a miraculous comeback were dashed after an hour when Swindon went 4-2 ahead. Midway through the second half Steven Davies brought one back for United but with six minutes remaining the home side scored their fifth.

With two minutes left Matthew Dunne made it 5-4, then in the final minute Ched Evans levelled the scores on the night. Seven minutes of time were added on but United couldn't find the goal that would have forced extra time.

The 5-5 scoreline and 7-6 aggregate are both play-off records. United also earned another unwanted statistic with the defeat, making it eight play-off participations without being promoted, a record they share with Brentford.

When Regan Slater scored in an EFL trophy tie at Grimsby on 9th November 2016, he beat Simon Stainrod's record as Sheffield United's youngest scorer in any competition.

With promotion being United's main aim, they had not taken the EFL Trophy too seriously. There were just 597 fans present at Blundell Park and no matter what the result, neither side had any chance of making the knockout stages.

United's manager Chris Wilder named a side almost entirely of Academy players. Slater was one of those, making his debut at the age of 17 years and 60 days.

At half-time United trailed 1-0 but in the 53rd minute Slater equalised with a well driven finish. He went on to complete the whole ninety minutes as United went on to win the game 4-2.

Slater's strike meant he had beaten Stainrod's record as the club's youngest scorer in any competition by just one day. However Slater's United career has not progressed in the same way that Stainrod's had. Since then he has made only two further appearances for United, both in 2017-18. He spent the following two seasons on loan at Carlisle and Scunthorpe respectively.

2017
THE BOUNCING DAY
MASSACRE

The Steel City Derby of 24th September 2017, in which Sheffield United beat Sheffield Wednesday 4-2 at Hillsborough, will forever be remembered by Blades fans as the 'Bouncing Day Massacre'.

Goals from John Fleck and Leon Clarke put the Blades 2-0 up after just fifteen minutes, but on the stroke of half-time Wednesday pulled a goal back to give them hope for the second half.

In the 65th minute a thunderbolt strike from Lucas Joao sent the home fans wild. They then did a bouncing celebration that was still going on two minutes later, only coming to a halt when they sensed danger from Mark Duffy's run into the area. Duffy scored from a tight angle and United's celebrations included singing "You're not bouncing anymore".

Clarke added another in the 77th minute and the game finished 4-2. It was the first time that United had scored four goals at Hillsborough.

For years Wednesday fans had taunted their cross city rivals about their 4-0 victory in the fixture at Hillsborough on Boxing Day 1979, which became known as the Boxing Day Massacre. Now United fans could hit back with taunts of a massacre of their own.

2017
CHAMPIONS OF ALL
FOUR DIVISIONS

When Sheffield United were promoted in 2016-17 with a club record points haul, they became the first English side to finish champions of all four divisions.

Former Blades defender Chris Wilder was appointed as manager replacing Nigel Adkins. He was mainly limited to free transfers for bringing players in and appointed lifelong fan Billy Sharp as captain.

After four games, nobody could have foresaw what was to come as United were bottom of the table with just one point. However a home victory over Oxford United on 27th August was the first of a fifteen game unbeaten run that lifted them into the play-off positions.

A home defeat to Walsall on 29th November failed to stop momentum and the Blades responded with six straight wins, going top of the table with victory over Northampton on New Year's Eve.

United had a slight wobble in the middle of January, failing to win in three games. After that they were unbeaten in their last seventeen games. Promotion was clinched with four games to spare and they finished the season as champions with their best ever tally of 100 points.

In finishing as champions of the third tier for the first time in their history, the Blades had become the first English team ever to win all four divisional titles.

2019
PROMOTION TO
THE PREMIER LEAGUE

Promotion to the Premier League was secured in 2018-19, edging aside Leeds United to the second automatic spot.

Despite the sale of David Brooks to Bournemouth, manager Chris Wilder made some shrewd signings. Without a net spend, he put together an effective side made up entirely of players from the British Isles.

Wilding deployed an effective 3-4-1-2 formation. The use of wing backs allowed United to dominate the opposition when attacking, but three central defenders made them solid defensively. The last line of defence, keeper Dean Henderson, who was on loan from Manchester United and never played at Championship level, was a revelation.

Things got off to a slow start with United losing their first two games, but they then won four in succession to take them into the promotion places. They remained there all season and from New Year were never out of the top three.

On 16th March The Blades beat Leeds 1-0 at Elland Road to move into second place, above their Yorkshire rivals. Promotion was as good as secured in the penultimate game of the season, when Ipswich were beaten 2-0 at Bramall Lane.

The following day things became mathematically certain when Leeds could only draw with Aston Villa. Wilder described United's promotion as "an incredible feeling for everybody connected with the club".

2020
FACT 99
TRANSFER RECORD
BROKEN AGAIN

After adapting well to life in the Premier League, United broke their transfer record during the January 2020 window.

Unlike the two other sides promoted with them, The Blades more than held their own during the first half of the season and by January had hopes of European qualification.

Before the season started, United had smashed their transfer record when they paid £20 million to Swansea City for centre forward Oli McBurnie. A day before the January transfer window closed, they brought in twenty-one-year-old Norwegian midfielder Sander Berge from Belgian side Genk.

Berge had spent three years playing for Genk and appeared for them in the Champions League during the first half of 2019-20. Despite his young age he had already been capped twenty times by his country.

Although not formally disclosed, the fee was acknowledged to be a club record and widely reported to be £22 million. Manager Chris Wilder told the club's official website: "I think this signing just shows how far we have come in a short space of time, that we are now attracting the likes of Sander to the football club. It's a brilliant signing for us."

Although Sheffield United exceeded all expectations in 2019-20. there was a feeling of what might have been if the Hawkeye goal line technology and VAR officials had shown some common sense on 17th June 2020.

The Blades were seventh in the table and dreaming of European qualification when the Premier League was suspended in March due to the Coronavirus pandemic. When it resumed behind closed doors three months later, United were involved in the first fixture, away to Aston Villa.

In the first half, Villa keeper Orjan Nyland clearly carried the ball over his own goal line, but the referee's watch did not receive a signal to say it had been a goal. Unbelievably the VAR officials did not step in to look at the incident, on the basis that they could only intervene to review goals.

At halftime it was confirmed that the Hawkeye system was working, with the explanation given that all seven cameras had been obscured. United had to settle for a draw and they lost their next two games.

The Blades eventually finished ninth and Chris Wilder was runner up to Liverpool's Jürgen Klopp in the Manager of the Year awards. It was still United's joint highest position since 1975, but things may have turned out even better had they beaten Villa.

The 100 Facts Series

Player Autographs

Player Autographs

Player Autographs

Player Autographs

Player Autographs